FROM THE TENEMENT
WINDOW

FROM THE TENEMENT WINDOW

A Selection of Glasgow Poetry and Prose
by Carolyn Carroll

Illustrated by Stephen Jeffreys

DEDICATION

This book is dedicated to my daughters Joanne,
Frances, Angela and Catherine and to my
husband Peter who took me from an outside
toilet to a home with two toilets!

CHRISTMAS

It was in nineteen fifty-eight when Scotland first made Christmas Day a bank holiday. New Year was the big celebration with Hogmanay traditions being carried on religiously in almost every home.

However, our house like many more was different. Christmas was as important as New Year and from as far back as I can remember there was always a Christmas tree, presents, church and Christmas dinner which always included our grannies' fun, laughter and games, just like most of the families who lived in the Glasgow tenements.

Living in a tenement, with only a room and kitchen there was only one place to put up the tree and that was at the window that faced on to the street. For us, that was our

bedroom, this was where the mahogany dressing table stood, normally in front of the oriel window. The big mirror was unscrewed and placed carefully behind the dresser, leaving a perfect piece of furniture to hold our tree in the best spot.

My dad, a cable maker, always bought the Christmas tree on the way home from work, at the last minute, usually on Christmas Eve, when they were at their cheapest.

My two sisters and I were beside ourselves with excitement by the time he arrived home. I stood impatiently at the tenement window ready to shout.

" Georgie, Isobel, dad's coming down the street. Look at the size of the tree he's carrying"

We knew he would always buy the biggest one he could carry. We loved when it touched the ceiling and at times bent its head as it was just too big for the room.

Dad wedged it into the coal bucket with big lumps of coal, mum held it to straighten it.

The old bucket was covered with colourful Christmas paper, bits of trimmed branches were placed around it to finish with and we stood in awe thinking we were the luckiest girls in the world with the most beautiful Christmas tree ever.

I'll never forget the smell of those trees. My dad brought the forest home to us that night. We could smell the woods, mountains and the clean fresh air in that wonderful tree.

Now all we had to do was decorate it.

When the big cardboard shoebox with the decorations was brought down from the shelf in the cupboard, we carefully unwrapped all the wee glass baubles and dad dealt with the fairy lights.

I don't remember even one year when those lights worked first time. Dad usually had to run out there and then still in his work clothes to Woolworths before it closed to buy replacements bulbs. We all held our breaths as he screwed them in and switched them on to test if they worked. Voila! Once more he had those precious lights working.

The fairy lights were put on the tree first and switched on. Oh, those beautiful wee lights. I stood back mesmerized by them as they shone through the dark tree branches like glowing fairies making their way through a night- time forest.

We all had a hand in hanging the decorations. Fragile colourful baubles, wee painted Santa's, tiny toys, homemade paper lanterns and finally the star. As I was the youngest I was lifted up to place this on the top of the tree. We stood for ages, the whole family, just soaking in our magnificent tree. How special were those moments?

Dad had made a stable out of cardboard for the nativity figures. A dark blue background with silver stars, cotton wool on the roof for snow and sprinkled with silver glitter which sparkled as the fairy lights shone on it. Straw on the floor and a small manger. Before all the figures were placed in it, he made a hole at the top of the back and pulled a fairy light through to light up the nativity scene.

Our tree was ready to join the legion of trees that stood at every window of every house in our street.

Each night as I turned into my street I was given a magical pathway home. An explosion of light replaced the grey stones of the tenement buildings and all those Christmas trees in all those windows transformed our street into our own wonderful colour filled forest.

CHRISTMAS TREES

Turning the corner my heart lights up
Each window winks at me
For fairy lights a child's delight
Dress up the Christmas trees

Each tenement window parades its' own
And decorates the street
My eyes absorb this wondrous sight
Heart memories to keep.

WINTER

During the winter it was so cold in a tenement. There was no central heating so the house was freezing and getting up in the morning required sheer grit and determination, and sometimes we got dressed in bed.

In the fifties most houses were heated by coal fires which had to be cleaned out set and lit. Sometimes there would be a wee electric two bar fire that kids would huddle round whilst taking their breakfast.

Ice formed around the inside of windows creating lace-like patterns and draughts like gales blew in from every nook and cranny. Character forming, I believe-if you survived.

My father like my granny used to pile the fires up high so that when on, they really did radiate through our house. Sometimes my dad, who had been in the fire service during the war would set the chimney alight (in a controlled way he told my mum) to clear all the built- up soot. Not everyone could afford a chimney sweep and we were on the top floor after all.

On terribly cold nights dad would take a shovel full of hot coals and hurry with them through the lobby to our room, where he would throw them onto the fire and start one for us. In no time he would have a roaring fire going, to heat the room where we slept.

After mum had supervised us being washed and in our pyjamas, we'd jump into bed. The three of us sisters slept in the one set in bed, two at the top and one at the bottom and always a foot in your face. Then my dad would heat our sheets and blankets and throw them over us. What a feeling when that hot flannelette sheet floated down over us, that was love and pure luxury.

WINTER

A Memory

In the cold of winter
In that tenement high
Ice inside my window
Bedtime nigh

No chill for me this evening
Sheets warmed by the fire
Father throws them gently
Over as we lie

Gazing through a curtain
From the set-in bed
Our room is filled
With glowing embers
Memory held inside my head

WINTER STREETS

We had one of the most amazing streets. My dad had told me that it was an Italian designed road surface which had been used, hence the smooth hard almost terrazzo effect, granite in concrete then polished to give a smooth surface. This was the best for all sorts of games especially roller skating. Remember in the fifties very few people owned cars particularly in our tenements, so playing in the street was quite safe.

The best thing, for a child living in a tenement was the number of other kids that were around to play with. So, there was no shortage when rustling up a rounders team, two sides for kick the can or organizing a back-street concert.

Best of all during the winter after a heavy snowfall we would all gather together in the early evening for snow fights and slide making. Oh, the joy of dark nights, lamplight, snow falling and all of us screaming and laughing.

WINTER STREET

The moon shines on an excitement of snow
Whilst youths with breaths like dragons
Make hasty efforts to build and slide and throw
Their joyous shouts ring out
As street lights catch their dancing shapes
For magic nights like these are rare
As snowflakes drift through frozen air

Don't call don't ask me to come now
I want to stay till dawn
To make my print on streets of white
As nature does in early morn
And gaze as flake on flake arrives
Caught up in floating hypnotize
To stand and wonder, oh perfect night
Keep memory, this child's delight

BACKCOURTS

A lot happened in the back courts of tenements. They were incredibly busy places. Along with the nineteenth century built tenement came the wash houses where fires were stoked under metal boilers set in brick. The women used to boil their clothes, finish with a thorough wash in the great big tubs then use a hand ringer to squeeze out the water before drying them out on the line.

There were pre-arranged times for the use of these wash houses and agreements about whose turn it was to hang out their rope for drying. Washing and hanging out clothes was an art. You would be the talk of the street if your washing wasn't pristine white, then if it wasn't hung out properly.

Eventually the "steamie" took over from these wash houses and soon because of disuse and neglect they became great hiding places for all sorts of street games.

It's important to tell you that attached to each of these wash houses were the "midgies" not the flying kind but the place where all household rubbish that wasn't burned in the fire was tipped into bins, around the bins, in front of the bins till it was pouring out of the midden.

This rubbish tip was an Aladdin's cave to the young children where bits of rope, jars and bottles along with a million other things could be found and when a game of kick the can was decided, the challenge was to see who could retrieve the best can from the midden.

Young children played in the back courts under the watchful eye of family or neighbours.

In the summer kids would lie on top of the dykes as they were called to swap comics especially American ones and a favourite game though many a child was impaled whilst trying their hand at it was jumping from dyke to dyke wall to dyke. I believe this could have been the fore runner to Parkour. Often I would lie just looking up to the sky figuring out the shapes in the clouds and pretending I was somewhere else.

One of the best things held in back courts was a concert.

Adults helped but generally the older children organized, made the costumes, decided who was in it and got in touch with the Daily Record's Pat Roller (patroller) to give him the money they would collect for charity. Crepe paper in all colours shaped at the bottom by wee fingers, white bows stitched on, along with sequins, sandshoes decorated and rehearsals in the close for weeks before.

Mums and dads, grannies and neighbours pulled out all the stops to add to these events.

Chairs were brought out, treats were made for selling and the odd Brownie camera was made ready for photographs.

BACK COURT CONCERT

They've practiced songs and dancing now
Crepe paper outfits on the stairs
The word's got round it's Howat Street
For Thursday night's affair

Back concert signs are posted up
Jean's mother's made the peas
The chairs are round the rope is too
Grannies set at ease

The audience at last are hushed
To hear the song and dance
The skaters waltz is played out loud
Excited children take their chance

Hot peas with dark brown vinegar
Served from a low-down house
Puff candy made by Jim Mc Leod
Leave sticky traces round the mouth

The main event the coup d'état
Is sung, applause is over
Cans go round, it's always done
Donations to Pat Roller

TENEMENT LIFE

A tenement house usually meant that your home consisted of a room and kitchen with a toilet on the landing shared with two other families.

Generally, the mum and dad slept in the kitchen and the children slept in the room.

Our kitchen was where we ate, talked, listened to music, washed ourselves, did our homework. Where the ironing was done and where visitors were given a cup of tea or a meal. It was a multi-purpose room. The set-in bed was high and allowed stuff to be stored under it (space was at a premium). It housed things such as my father's tool box, (by the way our Christmas presents were hidden in this box and when my mum and dad went to the pictures we scoured the house searching for any presents. Of course even a glimmer of them in the tool box stopped us looking further, we felt we had overstepped the mark covered up our search and retreated back to our books and games.)

There was the tin bath for our Friday night baths, shoes and at Christmas the big sweet jars that were fermenting the home -made sherry for New Year and a plenty of other collectables!

The bedroom also had a set-in bed. My friend slept looking up at her dad's bike which was suspended by a pulley above her. The three of us girls slept in the one bed, till the oldest was given the joy of her own bed in the form of a bed settee.

Apart from a wardrobe, armchairs and a dressing table we had a piano. My father was able to thump the piano and knock out a tune. Parties were a regular feature in our lives there was nothing like a get together with a good sing song and everyone had to have a party song ready.

On some occasions a neighbour from across the street (a true pianist) would be invited over to play. This would allow my dad to do what he did best sing all night.

On rainy days if children didn't play in the close at shops, dressing up, houses or with games you would more than likely end up in your own house doing something like staring out of the window.

Luckily enough our bedroom looked over Fairfield's Shipyard wall which then had was very low. From there past the shipyard you could see the Clyde with all the ships sailing up and down and further on over to the north side Glasgow University. It was never boring looking out of that tenement window, never.

MY FORTRESS

The pyramid blocks that encase my domain
The smooth flat slate tiles shiny slides for the rain
The black chimney pots, with life they exude
The remnants of coal or some work stolen wood

A cave in the storm, my bed with three walls
A but and a ben linked by one dark short hall
A place that is safe where space is confined
That wraps itself round you that's warm that's kind

Windows that stretch to catch all the light
Let gentle street shadows pervade in the night
A door roughly varnished, wide combed straight and curled
Holds a key in the lock to welcome the world.

FROM THE TENEMENT WINDOW

There are times I feel sad in my tenement home
I want mountains to climb and green fields to roam
There are times when the sound of a train makes me ache
For that place far away for that euphoric state
There are times when my soul wants to leap from within
And fly over houses and cranes and the din
Of the chatter of people, the welders loud drone
To be free from a life in a tenement home.

DREAMS

I've stood at this window many times
Above Fairfield's brick wall
And dreamed of places far from here
From tenements dark and tall

Only a glimpse of the river I see
But yet it moves me so
As boats sail up so quietly
As ferries come and go

A world out there so different
From anything on my street
Wild exotic countries
These ships all sail to meet.

TENEMENT COUNTRY

Lazy hazy days of summer
Spent on a concrete dyke
No trees or fields to rest my eyes
No sounds of nature or no sights
Only this patch of God's blue sky
Framed by four great walls
Allows me to dream of the shapes in the clouds
And watch as the sunlight falls
On tenement squares with eyes of glass
That catch this picture I see
Reflecting its beauty in myriad forms
Kaleid-escaped world for me.

OUTSIDE TOILET

There were all sorts of outside toilets then. Some were actually outside and pretty horrific. Some were in the back close for the low-down houses. These were often a mess because no matter how hard the women in the close worked to keep them clean others would use them and leave them in a disgraceful state. How lucky was I, we lived on the top floor and had a key for ours?

Every week a family would take their turn to wash the stairs then the toilet. Can you imagine only once a week the toilet used by three families got a thorough cleaning. Vim, bleach, scrubbing brush, Dettol all used to make it useable again for the next week. Our toilet had no toilet paper we used torn up newspaper squares tied onto a nail with string. It also didn't have a light.

During the day this was no problem but come NIGHTIME well that was a different story.

You see I had an aunt Chrissie whom all my friends loved she used to gather us round in the close and tell us ghost stories. We loved her tales of the unexpected, but come time to go home and up our poorly lit stairs, we were all scared out of our wits. Aunt Chrissie had to walk everyone to their own door and see us home. Now I was filled with stories about Hairy Paws and The Green Glove!

As a child I would dread having to go down to our toilet at night. People used to talk about a bogie man, and I had my suspicion where it lingered.

THE OUTSIDE TOILET

I have an outside toilet,

Ten stone steps from our door.

Shared with two other families

It sits between two floors

No light hangs from its' ceiling

The seats scrubbed wood smooth white

No soft rolled toilet paper

A daunting place at night

In bed when all are sleeping

My young eyes open wide

As darkness hangs around me

A fear builds up in side

What lurks in there ten steps below

I'll wait if only I can

For if I visit in the night

I'm sure I'll meet the BOGIE MAN

HALLOWEEN

Halloween was always celebrated on the last Friday of October. Why the Friday? Well! that was "pay" night and the night you'd be most likely to be given a threepenny bit (my favourite coin) or a sixpence which opened up so many doors especially the front door of the Plaza cinema on a Saturday morning

Halloween was completely different then to how it is now. There were no big stores with dressing-up outfits so it was a case of what your mammy could find for you from the back of the wardrobe.

My granny Hogan a widow who was poor had kept from her young days, some long dresses, jet beaded bags and necklaces that were really quite beautiful. She allowed my sisters and I to dress up in them and if we took care, we could wear them at Halloween.

So when I wasn't dressed up as a chimney sweep I borrowed granny's dress, a bag and necklace and proud as punch ran down stairs to meet my pals. We all carried scooped out turnips with little candles inside. Their light shone through the cut out faces giving them a skull like appearance.

We set off round our local tenement houses to go "guising".

When we knocked on a door and asked "Anything for my Halloween?" the family would ask us in. We would have to have a party piece ready, maybe a song, a poem or tell a joke. I always sang I'm Forever Blowing Bubbles. Only then would we be given a treat. Usually fruit, nuts or sweets and sometimes a threepenny bit, that would be a big treat.

We always went out early evening, it would be dark, and also often very foggy which I loved because it added that air of ghostliness and mysteriousness to the atmosphere of that night.

When we had finished we'd hurry back home with our cache of goods in our wee bags and finish the night "dookin" for apples and eating candy apples.

HALLOWEEN

Set a scene for Halloween
A fog filled night
Subdued gas light
A quiet stillness soon erupts
With children's shouts "Come hurry up"
Dressed as tramps and half-baked witches
Their mother's skirts
Their daddy's breeches
Waistcoats hats and caps with skips
When put together do the trick
The lanterns made from turnips smell
As candles smoke the spooned- out shell
With cut out faces
Made to scare
They light the way through autumn air
"Come in, come in wee folk and sing
Is it a story or a highland fling
You know a turn is always done
Before your treats are fairly won"
Nuts, tangerines and sometimes sweets
From friendly homes in friendly streets
As by the close the mothers' call
Some wrapped in coats and some in shawl
To gather now their worn- out brood
And take them home for bed and food
But one last thing before they're scrubbed
"dookin" for apples in the old tin tub.

CLYDESIDE FOG

When nature pours out over towns
It's veil of fog and slows life down
Then green is lost from every park
And chimney pots are clothed in dark

Each child is held in God's own maze
For corner streets are out of gaze
A silence reigns for sound is held
Within this form where sound is quelled

The tramcars rattle now subdued
Their lights so dim and so diffused
In dreamlike state they slowly drift
Ghosts seen through this autumn mist

A quiet eeriness takes form
As grey clothed figures head for home
And children scramble up the stairs
To find their place by cosy hearths.

STREET LIFE

Our tenement street filled with single ends, room and kitchens, outside toilets, tiled closes   resembled a beehive pulsating with life and activity.

Many of the fathers worked in the shipyards or engineering works around or very near Govan. Many of the women worked in factories or shops. Grannies were enlisted to look after and help with small children and were very much a part of the extended family.

Because there were so many children around, it was always easy to find someone to play with and often big groups got together for a big two team rounders match. Children didn't go in and out of each others houses to play. If it was dry you played in the street, if it was wet you played in the close, usually at shops, schools or reading comics.

On good days, Elder Park was a favourite place to walk to and with its pond, swings, trees grass and flowers and even a sandpit at one time, it really was a great park to have nearby.

It was normal to borrow a football, roller skates and in some cases even a bike if you never had one. This I did and suffered the consequences.

THE BIKE

"Are you coming out now?"
"No! I fell off a dyke"
"Is your arm really broken?
Can I borrow your bike?"

You see the crowd's cycling to Renfrew just now
I'm sorry you can't come
But if you think it's alright
I'll take it just now
I'll return it tonight.
Your mum'll not mind
She knows I'm your friend
I'll be careful down hills
And round a sharp bend.

I'll pump up the tyres
It'll come to no harm
Thanks you're a real pal
Now, look after that arm

I'm back and I'm sorry
I fell from your bike
The wheel caught a stone
I went into fast flight
Right over the handles
Straight onto my face
I've buckled the wheel
and your paint works all grazed

I'll have to run now
You see I'm in pain
I think my arm's broken
My head's feeling strange
I'll probably get plastered
By "doc" and by dad
"How's your arm?"
Here's your bike
I'll pay it all back

You should have said, "No"
"Get lost Go away
You're not much of a friend
Wanting only my bike.
It never concerned you
I fell from a Dyke!"

GAMES

My theme park was Elder Park
My boats were lolly sticks
The sports I played were kick the can
With boys chase, catch and kiss

My superslides were made of ice
My ball games 'gainst a wall
The close a haven in the rain
My dress up clothes a shawl

THE SISTER'S GOFER

In the forties and fifties family life was simple. The family was an extended one with grandparents as it was in our case round the corner or a short walk away.

Aunts uncles and cousins were also a great part of our family and always seemed to be in our house for wee visits and impromptu parties.

There was no television for us till the late fifties so movies (which I couldn't get enough of) radio and reading books from Elder Park Library were the stimulus for our minds.

How great was it to stand in a queue waiting to see a movie. A British movie, a big American blockbuster Pathe news and the coming attractions all in the one night. Two films ! fantastic.

As I was the youngest of three sisters, I had to stand in the queue whilst my mum and dad washed up the evening dinner dishes and my older sisters finished off homework so we could all go out to the Lyceum Cinema.

There we would be taken into worlds we could only dream of, where stars were beyond reach and the splendor on screen took us on an exciting magic carpet ride that stayed with us as we went home and drifted into sleep.

I was the gofor for my sisters. Go for this, go for that.

But there was one thing I couldn't stand doing for them and that was to take their overdue books back to the library. It terrified me. The librarian held a revered position of authority. The kings and queens of that remarkable building.

Why is it every time I stepped into that library I instantly needed the toilet.

THE LIBRARY

I carried the hen basket for my sisters
Filled with their library books
They always made me do it
You see I was the youngest of the brood

I'd cry and argue and cause such a stir
But they'd laugh and say stop the fuss
This is what wee sisters do
They're supposed to run errands for us

I didn't mind running to Galls for their stockings
Or picking up things from the chemist, with care
I'd even stand in the Lyceum queue
While they took out their rollers and did up their hair

But the one thing I hated I really abhorred
Was when they insisted and made me "Go now"
To the Elderpark Library with books that they knew
Were more than a week and a half overdue.
For when I entered that temple of silence
The woman would shout as she looked at each book
"Overdue! Overdue, by such a long time
That everyone froze to turn round and look

At me the offender, whose head hardly reached
The mahogany counter where this judge loudly preached
'bout people who kept HER books for this time
Should be banned from the library and given huge fines.

My face was bright red as she ranted and raved
And all others nodded, as they stood and they gazed
But I knew the truth for each of them feared
That black headed woman with a hint of a beard

LIVING NEAR FAIRFIELDS

We lived in the shadow of Fairfield's Shipyard. One of its walls ran the full length of Taransay street. It wasn't very high at all in fact the men used to skip over it to sneak out for cigarettes during work hours. Because it was only about six or seven feet high it meant that I could have this great view from my third floor tenement window.

I loved Fairfields. The noises of the welders working night shift lulled me to sleep, their flashing light a comfort as it lit up the room where I slept. Something strong and constant in my young life.

The tall cranes peered over Govan like sentinals guarding all of its inhabitants. As they turned slowly lifting and moving their loads helping to build the ships on the Clyde they became one of the most steadfast and familiar sights of my youth.

Govan life was in tune with Fairfield's loud whistle.

It sounded in the morning, lunchtime and evening. Then Fairfield's big gates would open and droves of men in work clothes and "bunnets" would pour out till they were whistled back in.

It was a lively and busy time lots of jobs, and a future offering opportunity and prosperity.

FAIRFIELDS WHISTLE

The whistle has gone
It's five o'clock
The great gates open wide
The men rush out in droves
And soon there's emptiness inside

I set my clock by that loud scream
I pull my coat and run
To wait impatiently by doors
When everyone has gone

My rendez-vous my special place
Arranged where I shall meet
My dad who's coming home from work
I run. He sweeps me off my feet.

HOLIDAYS AT AYR

One of the oldest holidays in Scotland the Glasgow Fair dates back for hundreds of years. It was the time when everything in Glasgow closed shipyards, factories even offices. It allowed folk to take a trip to the seaside or have days out or go "doon the water"

We went by bus to Ayr. The pram, the case, towels and bedding travelled by train and was collected from the station after we arrived. I oftened wondered why a pram travelled in luxury yet we waited in a mile long queue for the bus that I was always sick on.

I had two wee cotton dresses made by a local dressmaker, new white sandshoes and socks, ribbons and a swimsuit in preparation for our summer holiday. Post war swimsuits weren't gorgeous still I loved my crinkle stretch muddy green little one My sisters were airforce blue and after ten minutes in the cold cold sea it was difficult to tell where their blue legs stopped and the blue swimsuit started.

Our mum and dad aunts and uncles all went paddling. Men with trousers rolled up showing their white bony legs and the women with their skirts and dresses tucked up in their knickers. They laughed and jumped about in the water like children, unusually carefree and liberated.

Oh! I nearly forgot about granny Hogan, dressed in a black coat and hat settled in her deckchair clasping her black leather bag. She didn't laugh a lot just absorbed the scene as she ate her ice-cream cone.

And usually it rained!

HOLIDAYS AT AYR

Thank God for Woolies down at Ayr
Our favourite shop for sure
We'd run in there for plastic macs
Drenched from that sudden downpour

With hoods and matching belts as well
What choice! Pink green or blue
I loved the smell, it's crunchy feel
The thrill it was see-through

ON THE BEACH

We did wear swimsuits
Funny things
All crinkled with no flowers
Granny sat with hat and bag
While we built sandy towers

They did go in the water
With skirts tucked up a bit
And trousers rolled 'bove pale skinned knees
That salty waters licked

We jumped and screamed
As we raced in
And cold waves found our bodies
The Brownies clicked
That moment kept with others stored
In cupboards deep in lobbies.

HOGMANAY

New year was the big celebration. For a long time it was the winter holiday long before Christmas held it's rightful place as a work's holiday. What a time Hogmanay and New Year were. My mum and dad had their own special way to prepare for this great occasion which started months before.

Apart from the odd sherry my parents didn't drink alcohol, yet for each New Year they always made their own homemade sherry using an old family recipe. Instead of taking many months even years to age this brew was ready in a few months. I haven't got the recipe, rightly or wrongly, I never asked for it.

However my memory is of sultanas, sugar, yeast, water, big screw top sweetie jars and must not forget mum's freshly washed stockings (for straining the mixture). These jars were left to ferment, of all places, under mum and dad's set-in bed in the kitchen, which was dark deep and held so many other things there. Space was at a premium in a room and kitchen so "under the bed" was a great area to put the tin bath, the one we girls had our weekly bath in and which also doubled up as mum's container for the weekly washing when she went to the "steamie".

One of the other rituals for this special time of the year was the grocery club. Galbraiths was the shop mum had hers. Every week for months a couple of shillings was paid in, recorded in a wee book and left to mount up till New Year. When dad walked in with that cardboard box of food and took out each item to let us see what had been bought we really couldn't believe we could have such amazing treats.

Madeira cake, sultana cake, shortbread, nuts, biscuits, fresh butter shaped with wooden paddles and finished off with a thistle design and in amongst all of these was a little jar of maraschino cherries. Everybody hated the taste of them but they did look posh if someone had a snowball cocktail or a Babycham.

Apart from food there were many more rituals. All curtains and clothing had to be washed along with windows, floors and the stairs and all bins emptied. Often kitchens were re-wallpapered, doorsteps whitened, sometimes front doors revarnished and a pattern made with an old strong comb, kids bathed, clothes changed, clootie dumplings made and ginger wine.

Finally a pristine tablecloth was laid with all the food, drinks and glasses set out ready to welcome the New Year in along with the first footers.

HOGMANY

A table laid with crisp white cloth
A spread of cake and shortbread tails
Welcome all the neighbours to
The food, the talk, whilst bagpipes wail

Windows open keys in doors
Revellers come and stay
A circle forms with rousing lilt
That well known chant for New Years day

A glass is raised, a hand is held
A light kiss on the cheek
A hopeful look to more good times
A wish your "lum will always reek"

THE STEAMIE AND HOT BATHS

The washhouses in the backcourts became disused and derelict, when the Steamie opened it's doors to the Govan woman.

What a place! In the same building were swimming pools and hot baths, where hot water was provided by a shift of men continually shovelling huge amounts of coal into great furnaces. They were run by Glasgow's corporation to provide for the community at a reasonable price, a facility where they could swim, have a hot bath and wash large amount of laundry whilst SOCIALISING. You notice I put that word in capitals, for a very good reason.

The women would gather all the household clothes, bedding, curtains, towels, shirts, dresses, underwear and anything else they could lay her hands on. Pile it high into a big tin bath, put it on an old pram and push it all the way up to the steamie, often dragging along an older child to help get the load along the road.

The "wean" would then be allowed to go to the swing park across the road till mum or granny were finished.

In all honesty, the women didn't want the child to hear the conversations that went on inside.

No one needed to visit a psychologist then because all problems were aired, as they washed and rubbed and scrubbed with their old wood and zinc scrubbing boards. These women in their patterned peenies and hair caught up in turbans talked about their husbands, weans, illnesses, menages but oh, how they laughed as they shared these stories. There was a real sense of empathy and solidarity.

On a Friday night everything changed. The "steamie" was closed and the hot baths became the gathering place. As tenements weren't blessed with toilets in the house then, a bathroom was certainly not found in many tenements.

The weekly bath for most adults took place there on a Friday night. One area for men and one for ladies. Most were getting ready for the weekend when the factory girls prepared for the big nights out at the dancing. Those girls really did have a dramatic change. During the week overalls, turbans and little makeup, they transformed into beauties. Beautiful dresses, hairdos, carefully applied makeup perfume and high heels. In Glasgow there was a saying "you scrub up well" and the Glasgow girls did.

Every bath was in a cubicle and the bath attendant scrubbed the bath between each visit, then filled them up with, clean hot water at the perfect temperature. The next girl with her bag of soaps and towel then went in when called.

Just as the steamie was the perfect place for the married and the older woman to share their stories, gossip, joys and sorrows, so the hot baths were for the young women. The banter that was heard from each of these cubicles was vivid, intimate and informative. As a young teenager I didn't need a book or that talk about life, because all was revealed as the steam rose, the perfume filled the place and the conversations became as hot as the water.

MAMMIE AT THE STEAMIE

She loaded our bathtub to overflowing
With turbaned hair and grey coat flowing
She pushed the pram that once held me
Up Harhill Street to the local steamie

She joined the bustle of other women
Who stood to wash at stalls they were given
Whilst scrubbing and rubbing they blethered and havered
And laughed and joked but their job never wavered

I played in the park till she finished that day
And walked with her home holding hands on the way
'cause downhill was easy with that heavy load
For the tired out mum in her grey flannel coat

AUTUMN

I never really noticed autumn
Or when the leaves began to fall
I never heard the sounds of birds
Or recognise their different call
I never saw the hedgerow bloom
From the tenement window in my room

I noticed coats pulled tightly up
And cold creep from the Clydeside flow
I felt a darker damper night
And fog that masked all things from sight

I never really noticed autumn
As nature didn't lie close by
I never kicked the golden leaves
No fields and forests 'round tenements high

I'd watch the rain glide down my window
I'd play up closes, sit on stairs
I'd know that days had seemed to shorten
But I never, ever, noticed autumn

AUTHOR'S BIO

Carolyn Carroll's first collection of prose and poetry has been inspired by her most personal and poignant childhood memories of Govan, where she grew up with her mother, Myra, her father, James, and her two older sisters, Georgina and Isobel.

She moved to London from Glasgow when she was 27 and currently lives in Surrey with her husband, Peter and is surrounded by her family, grandchildren and friends. They raised their four daughters here, while Carolyn enjoyed a successful teaching career, inspiring many children over the years.

Printed in Great Britain
by Amazon

34278779R00030